Ice Walk

by Cass Hollander
illustrated by Bob Dorsey

MODERN CURRICULUM PRESS
Pearson Learning Group

"We had better head back," said Pa.
He looked at his watch. "It's getting
late. We want to be across the river
and home before dark."

   A trip across the river in winter was
a special outing for George and Nellie.
In spring, summer, and fall, they took
the ferry across. But in winter, the river
froze over. Then they walked right
across on the ice. It was more fun than
a playground.

It was March. Soon the ice would melt. But not yet! It was still cold. The ice was still hard as a rock. Even so, the family had to look out for cracks and breaks.

Pa and George led the way to the river. Nellie and Ma followed. At the river's edge, they met a man with a suitcase. He had come from the train station on the other side. Pa hailed him and asked about the ice.

"Solid as land," said the man. "I could have bounced a basketball on it!"

"Then let's be on our way," said Pa.

Then they aimed for the other side.

Pa and George stepped onto the ice. They went across first. Pa liked to go first. He wanted to be sure it was safe for the whole family.

George tried to match Pa's long steps. In no time, they were far ahead of Ma and Nellie.

Nellie didn't want to hurry. She loved being on the river. She liked to look at the sky and watch the clouds. With Pa up ahead, she felt sure the ice was safe.

"Are we to the middle yet?"
asked Nellie.

Ma stopped and looked from one
side of the river to the other. "I believe
we're already past it," said Ma. "But
come along. We must not make
Pa wait."

Ma took Nellie's hand, as they
aimed for the other side.

Just then they heard an awful groaning sound. The ice was starting to crack behind them! Was it starting to melt?

Nellie went stiff with fear. Ma did not let go of Nellie's hand. "We'll be fine if we keep going," she said.

Ma moved with long, strong steps,
She was almost pulling Nellie across
the ice. Nellie's heart bounced. She
could hardly breathe. She began
to cry.

Behind them, the groaning and creaking got louder and louder. It was like some awful thing chasing them across the ice. Nellie tried to see how close the breaks were, but Ma told her, "Don't look back!"

And so they crossed the river. At times they were just a step ahead of the cracks breaking up the ice.

As they got closer to the shore, Ma relaxed her grip on Nellie's hand. Then she slowed her pace as she aimed for the land. The danger was behind them. The ice was solid here.

Pa and George came out to meet them. "It's about time you got here," Pa said. Then he saw Ma's face and Nellie's tears. His own face went pale.

"The ice is not safe," Ma said simply. "It's starting to crack. The breaks are growing. We must spread the word."

Pa hailed a policeman and told him, "The ice is not safe." The policeman stayed by the river. He would warn people not to cross.

George went to the train station and told the station master, "The ice is not safe. It is starting to melt." The station master telegraphed the warning across the river.

No one else crossed the river that night. In fact, no one crossed for weeks—not until the river was clear of ice and the ferry could run again.